A Story of a Starseed

Poetry Blog: www.amazulugaming.com
Instagram: Onepoeticgamer
Twitch: www.twitch.tv/onepoeticgamer

© 2025 Billy Williams, Jr. All rights reserved, including the right to reproduce this book or portions thereof in any form whatsoever. Contact AmaZulu Gaming, LLC for info at the following e-mail: onepoeticgamer@amazulugaming.com

ISBN 979-8-9857102-3-6

Published by
AmaZulu Gaming, LLC

Cover Art by
Billy Williams, Jr.

Logo Designs by
Istimyouleye
Christopher James Rowland

Final Edition
Printed in the United States of America

Table of Contents

Side A

On The Way Here………………….....6
#believe………………………….....7
Poetical Enigma………….......……...9
It's Only Wordplay……………....…11
R-Evolve……...……………………..13
Matrix Ascension…….....…………..14
That's Peace…………….....………..16
To Be Loved…....…….……....……..18
Cosmic Thought……......…………...20
When The Traffic Stops….....………21
More Than a Word……....…….…...25

-DEFCON 1-

Side B

30……………….....……..Just a Matter of Time
32…………………….....……..Twin Flames
33…………………….....Two Eyes, No Lies
36………………………….....Currant Seed
38………….…........….....Came Here For This
40……………………….....………..Vortex
42………....,,,,....Where I'm Suppose to Be
43……………………….....Restoration
46……………………….....Remembering
49…………………………….....Oh Snap
51………………………….....Incarnate

Preface

I wrote this for me…

…for her…

…for us.

Side A

On The Way Here

Why does this feel familiar
moving past these stars and things
awakening and yet still caught in a dream
it seems like, I should call that one a moon
words I'm not use to feel limited
is this the experience I thought it would be
looking back I'm wondering if I took the
wrong route, guided post signs make it so self-doubt
is kept to a minimum
wait I think I see the sun
and that green and blue dot
that has to be the one,
I'm almost there
and it appears I'm right where I belong
the vibe is right, the frequency is like
just what I read about when studying the records
and just for a second
I process the word homesick
but, I'm not even there yet
or, what was that…
these thoughts are clumsy
it's like some thing is awakening
but I can't remember nothing
keep forgetting something
maybe, I'm living in a dream
and before I can connect the dots between
I can hear a baby scream…

#believe

Believe,
thinking of what I've achieved
conceived dreams in the sub-conscious
raised temps a couple of degrees
believe,
what's not seen I create by my own means
which means my imagination is quite keen
faith in what's not seen
it seems, if you believe
you wean off all doubts
applied pressure so I could let off steam
deem it more important to dream dreams
instead of listening
to anyone not on my team
believe,
meditate blues into greens
images worth imagining
written since I was thirteen
I sing, lyrics from my spirit
for souls that choose to hear it
stories from those silenced
can now make an appearance
use to worry about the small things
but that noise is incoherent
I cook up masterpieces in a skillet
so you can feel this flow to your spirit
as it's, far from detrimental
no place for designed hate
as deep down I'm sentimental
writing words to instrumentals

picture the impossible in my mental
keep it simple baby boy
brainwaves flowing from my temple
assemble, this verse a cappella
because these words I believe,
thinking of what I've achieved
conceived dreams in the sub-conscious
raised temps a couple of degrees
believe,
what's not seen, I create by my own means
which means my imagination is quite keen
faith in what's not seen
it seems, if you believe.

Poetical Enigma

Hourglass Nebula
Nikola Tesla
eye watching God
this is something that's irregular
different type cellular
poetic type molecular
lost religion so I'm secular
black sheep, that's one hell of a
interstellar, irregular
moving deep behind the retina
kind of clever huh
thoughts scribed on a tabula
then set on curricula
this has to be the
po-et, re-set, I bet
on black, like that
is fact, why ask
impact-ful verse
worth more than a high-end purse
I'm in my bag
but what's worse
made a gift from a curse
introvert in reverse
came back one more time
so the last could go first
circling the galaxy, traversed
my girth, immersed
only hurts when coerced
guess I shouldn't have jumped in headfirst
the enigma, now submersed

until the outburst dispersed
when conversed in this work
Poetic, from then to eternity well-versed
and I'm gone.

It's Only Wordplay

Throw this one up on hope
catch made is legendary
still be on my Tupac shit,
Hail Mary, carry thoughts electronically
specifically written in notes
spoken words from my Adam Apple
should I reference a Steve Job quote
tote lead legally
even when concealed
use of force, of course
leaks bloodwork from pen-cils
rit-u-als, done on task
spells casted poetically
you already know which craft
I mask, no it's not Halloween
so why ask
move past the ordinary
I guess I'm extra
son of the preacher man
maybe I can bless her
sí, I prefer to stir
my tea with a lot of honey
yes sir, deter
my mind from such lust filled thought
brought love into the mix
not knowing the cost
caught feelings, sky the ceiling
now what's been taught
checks bounce on lies that shouldn't been bought

so I sought, counsel from powers
I heard was on high
only to realize the same source
is sitting side by side
with I, wait, I meant my
subconscious, still see with no eye
contact, clear leading when I fly
fulfilled requirements on applications
so rules no longer apply
try, measuring the effort
despite going the distance
free verse helped me write this with no resistance
existence has been extensive
for a guy labeled defensive
pretense was intensive
is that why I'm so apprehensive
forgive this, forgive that
so please forgive me
forgive the hate that caused it in the first place
love coming in second so secondly
I do some things unexpected
except when he
accepts the third person
speaking in his mind indefinitely
I'm definitely different
wonder what she has to say
metaphor so many reasons
maybe she'll like my word play.

R-Evolve

360 degrees
full circle, revolving around
what's meant to be
I thought
then stopped
cleared space to clearly see
pushed from the left
and moved right into
eternity,
universally gleamed
shine bright in dark dreams
balance out coincidences
then call it
synchronicity,
eventually it will hit ya
if you miss just what I mean
what's meant to be
revolves around
full circle
see.

Matrix Ascension

She smelled of love
with a taste of happiness
and with feels like these he knew then
magic had become him,
so with a scientific explanation
he created words that required an education
for life to stand on
or maybe under
cause this is the ring around the roses
only these pockets aren't filled posies
they're filled with objects of affection
suggesting, matters of the heart
be taken into one's own hands
thinking, if the shared limits of
"dust to dust" can be moved past
we can touch down somewhere over the rainbow
somewhere that grass is greener
somewhere that expectations are set on nil
where creating can be enjoyed
and complacency is found in words like
love
truth
forever,
that "thing" beyond feeling
dealing in energy
that present in the moment
of what is, is
and he
spoke silence beautifully

viewed it outside of perspective
so then, she knew
the linguistics of math communicated
between the two
broke timelines built inside
the matrix.

That's Peace

Peace I seek
in the curves that meet
somewhere between magical feats
that serve as treats
peaked, my curiosity
the dichotomy
of innerstanding astronomy
describing the astrology
of your anatomy
eyes not meant to see
what a third feels in the belly
I rarely get the chance
to make sense ever since
an attempt to share depths
where nobody here has stepped
10,000 leagues under the sea
we're in our own, picture that
I take base in facts
bunkered in, buried next
to secrets kept
apart from where anyone is let
take the gamble to open if I knock
bet, text love in short stories
you can find in texts
explain how we can love forever
together, there won't be a need to guess
less is in fact more
studying to pass the test

cram all the info into a writing session
A plus one equals poetic
you know, the best
effects, from a butterfly
a cause for me to peek
enough tricks to trick a trickster
but I'd rather have the treats
that's magical, geometrical
feats that makes curves meet
from head to toe you're beautiful
and that's peace.

To Be Loved

This is what happens when
we experience beautiful,
can feel stars dance around us
while we hold hands
comfy in the company of the word love
sipping on timeless
laughing within the warmth of light
-this-just-might-be-
dream works in realty
the colors are more than I can mouth
so place your heart on my chest
and feel my soul beat
it's the divine in the air tonight
as a million eyes shine between us
screaming take the shot
I am because You are
as the witnesses ask
what's the catch
meditate until that sits
peacefully in rhythm at 528 hertz
this is craft on its job
and I appreciate the work
as such, appropriate to now mention
I'm never leaving this never land
-ever-
so let's let purity play
til our bones ache
with the feels this experience brings…

...I had seen her
was this in-between the
point of no return
and reoccurring dream we dreamed of...

Cosmic Thought

Universe
Spirit
God if you will,
names limited by consciousness
so let's move past logic builds
I need to make this connection
told to go inside and feel
feel the difference in meditation
faith activates for real
still hear the doubts talking
fear making moves to steal
until peace holds down uncertainty
rock steady on the water still
walking steady amidst the chaos
distractions have their appeal
anxiety awaits in a belly that aches
dark matters voice familiar appeals
but a trust distills
all worry that spilled
the path, untraveled but will
be blazed on
trails made from
cosmic thought
Allah
Yeweh
I am if you will.

When The Traffic Stops

It happened to someone's daughter
a mother, somebody's wife
hate induced fear beliefs
took the love from her life
I'm like…

It happened to someone's daughter
a mother, somebody's wife
hate induced fear beliefs
took the love from her life
I'm like…

I apologize for many things
even for what I've never done
love conquers hate in every case
as I contemplate the use of this gun
this son of man that got shit confused
cause the love of money in his heart
allows her to be used
abused, the unthinkable
how the hell could he choose
to hurt something so beautiful
it's all a lose lose,
as I lose what's left of me
hanging on to sanity
she fell into my arms a bloody mess
scarred forever actually
the facts you can't see
undermined by a man's belief

religion, power, pride leads
to a world that's full of grief
I seek to not forget it
as on my clothes her blood leaks
she speaks in such soft tones
I cry as vengeance I seek
want to say fuck peace
gritting my teeth, where's the relief
peep, I gotta eat this
so many bruises on her face
makeup won't make up
for excuses in this case
lies said consensual
words a law misplaced
she can't give consent under influences
they won't admit that it was rape
tape along the floor
where her body was placed
caused the "no" to echo loud
until the soul could get a taste
no, no, no, no, no…wait
you got to plate this
it was her experience
she tried to tell somebody she trusted
and they wasn't hearing none of it
told her toughin' up and shit
thought she was independent
bs from misguided stars
lead to this type of influence
I must have missed the notes
as she was choked by a member

of the family that held her close
in pictures, I don't remember
who let the fear take us to this place
I wish it was a bit simpler
him or her
well, it shouldn't even be a choice
like selling one's body just to live
evil backwards isn't reason to rejoice
moist eyes tell stories
traumatized, she made it through the drama
only to wish that she had died
realized she's unprotected
by those that claim to do so
society calls her names
like bitch, slut, stupid hoe
I don't know where to start
for her to begin to heal
steel willed
but what happens when the will's killed
feels different when this fills
one with so much pain
you think this world will
be a better place without your face
it's not a movie, this shit is real
when the traffic stops…

It happened to someone's daughter
a mother, somebody's wife
hate induced fear beliefs
took the love from her life
I'm like…

It happened to someone's daughter
a mother, somebody's wife
hate induced fear beliefs
took the love from her life
I'm like…

More Than a Word

Know that this isn't just a vibe
we speak energy
share memories that don't exist on timelines
finding ways to reach out and touch
despite never moving physically
essentially when it's that
belief you're in need of
like birds that fly above
that feeling of love was me
not for any reason other than
just because,
just because I can
because it's necessary
because I believe that the word friend
is such a beautiful and needed thing
that many claim they have
but more than enough can't say is true
and you…friend..
mean way more to me
than a word can ever define.

DEFCON 1

I gave my everything
or at least I thought I have
feel I have
stepping out of the last
experience that was sent
I was meant to do this
but, what is this
missed the points awhile back
watching minds relapse
acts not meant to move past old facts
odds stacked, bullshit tactics
fact is, I've come to grips with
she never loved me
they had to leave me
it had to be so I could see
a picture I snapped from a distant star
how far must I go
to be where you are
twin flame, one in the same
discovering why I came
here, in the first place
staring into myself when mirroring my face
erasing hate laced in this space
chased dreams seem displaced
replaced in case I'm given grace
so let's embrace,
get a taste of what it is to make
it happen, remember fact is
I've come to grips with
she never loved me
they had to leave me
it had to be so I could see
reality, actually
I'm seeing logic
correspondent that chose lyrical correspondence
different topics, pathologic

wordsmith giving this gift with a twist
roses from shit
fertilize and ferment
the noun type, sounds right
looks right
but comes from left field
willed to do more than use anger to kill
silently, since we've been programmed mentally
I disconnected only to reconnect
to the wisdom given originally
forgive me
as I forgive self
cue the dramatic horns
because this is the new way
to alert the masses it's DEFCON 1
and I've come from a distant dimension
fit in to learn the basic instructions
before I leave earth
giving everything I have
for what it's worth
on this rebirth
breaking an ancestral curse
no matter what they say in the verse
despite the fact I've been placed last
I shall…be one of the first.

Side B

Just a Matter of Time

She greeted me with, "Hey King."
I respond, "What's up Queen?"
and proceeded the conversation with..

No better way to script it
holding my golden ticket
soul chose to pick this
life, the school for my spiritual gifts
it's perspective shifted
unlearned hate invested
ancestral karma I borrowed
is now lifted
weight pushed up
chakra flexing
testing, the waters
the signs say I'm liquid
flows so filthy
where's the soap, out the box
make old look cool, that's vintage
I sip tea that's minted
create dreams vivid
things weren't always clear
before glasses I squinted
persisted, thinking I could write about life
hit the shop to get printed
fitted for the job
armor a bit dented
pens express universal love written
so what's missing

listen,
sounds of stars whispering in the night sky
feel the breath on my neck
from a precious butterfly
I, shine
when looking into your eyes
it's the moon sun effect
crescents on wings (angels)
we're on high
and, it's just a matter of time
golden ticket locked in my mind
soul chose to pick this
no better way to script it
brush off the ashes
phoenix arise.

Twin Flames

A kiss
even when metaphoric
is still a kiss
it's what we are
across the distance of infinite
energies held between
universal hands
spinning
the beginning
as if eyes are watching a god
create protostars
we are
merging into balance
chaotic love
craving experiences
that benefit
what we have to do
in time frames
designed for
twin flames.

Two Eyes, No Lies
(If Only You'd See)

I had seen her in passing
seen her move through
rear views of my school of thought
navigating its waves of commotion
emotions being made
as I gave pause to a sense of vision
lacking intuition initially
eventually, the inevitable happened
cause once play got pushed
the universe went to work
for what it's worth
there's no surprise we met soon after
as if opportunity contemplated
and decided this needed to happen
the questions I had been asking self
reflected this face to face
and despite her being laced with
the foundation of disguise
no amount of makeup could hide
or provide the intent meant to replace
perfection that I believed to be misplaced
with the mistakes I had made
dazed, in attempts to not judge
the cover of an unread book
had me thinking of another way to present
17-year-old feelings
that dwelled in the feminine aspects
like, how could I get
her to recognize this moves past skin deep

somewhere only a soul could peep
one so beautiful,
only for society to tell her no
don't even know
she's fighting against a whole situational cult
even when exposed
maybe if I spoke she could cope
with the facts that the truth lies
between belief in one's self
and the lies they give
as hope
no need to choke up about it
I doubt if the masses really care
tie dyed hair, should I dare
cause when she stares
I feel things like
"help", "hurt", "heal me for me"
is she even asking
or is this just a dream
one where I keep telling my conscious
shit really fertilizes flowers
this, sour taste in my mouth
this, bitter truth in my hands
I exchange for a key code
that could set us free
only to be, ostracized for being different
poked at because we attempt to fit in
to puzzle pieces already in place
for Christ's sake
it's a different world
then where my heart is coming from
trying to give her some

of this old school stardust
found in my pants pocket
that was left over from my youth
this truth of expression without the use of
codependent decisions
to narcissistic fundamentalists
here, she can take mutual benefits
and plug it into a dream not deferred
as I heard from miles away
that she didn't need another daddy
she just needed me to be
to exist and give pieces of authenticity
and eventually, it'll be whatever it is
as I spend the rest of my days boxing up
packages of faith, happiness and joy
deliver them to her doorstep as proof that
my two eyes have never lied
especially when staring back
at hers.

Currant Seed
(Currency)

She made way from the Philippines
bouncing on the balls of her feet
like waves she displayed
movements so beautiful
and if only for a second
I laid gracefully in the cusp of imagination
believing this currency was for me
this, piece of peace
momentarily gifted
positioned in parts of my mind on repeat
to nurture my malnourished system of trust
a now defunct subconsciousness
what's happening is
this is me two stepping with your silhouette
a sunny day with the dark side
mind's eye giving insight
to a view beyond the box
this must be where the unicorns play
since nobody will believe me anyway
let's say we do the unimaginable
what they call taboo
I'm guessing with all these thoughts
a penny for each
might not be worth much during inflation
unless, of course
there is no price on faith
on hope
on these two hands holding a heart
maybe you'll catch that

the second time around
you can find me somewhere lost
in love and lust
on the other side of the coin,
as luck would have it
I've flipped my lid
on this tale of tales
but, it all must mean something
maybe it's a one shot in a
parallel universe
and in this verse
she made way from the Philippines
bouncing on the balls of her feet
like waves she displayed
movements so beautiful
and, if only for a second
I laid gracefully in the
cusp of imagination
believing her currant seed was
for me.

Came Here For This

Safe space
played great
but you can't fake
programmed fate
until you
take space
make hate wait
touch love
and kiss faith in place
I reiterate
in outer space
I flow great
make the stars move and shake
we curved straight
run at a slow pace
unorthodox type weight
push of the chest plate
into a dead space
made live off this groove
the mood wakes
up, with no makeup
a cool drink
I sip from a dip in clear water
yup, soul moving and such
has me thinking luck
but knowing my trust
has more to do with my come up
shucks, it's a
safe space

came here for a taste
of the human experience
let's see what this lifetime
will make.

Vortex

Footprints left to avoid missteps
life spins quick inside a vortex
unstoppable forces mix within the cortex
move past presence when asking what's next.

Perception gives gift
when viewed differently,
as misunderstandings
can be united in a freedom
refusing to be boxed in
so, as I live with the constant
movement of ebb and flow
I go where the wind blows
unseen movement in cycles
particles amass
yet here I am whole
despite holes
black inside light
I invite all in
within my universe
made of multiple constituents
each part sharing in importance
that's perfect,
you should view this spectacle
in dimensional specs
while listening to love speak
stars wink by twinkling
in effort to keep hearts dreaming
a means found via medium

of life, that is
in its purest form
etched in ways
so it won't be mistaken
for anything less
it's…

Footprints left to avoid missteps
life spins quick inside a vortex
unstoppable forces mix within the cortex
move past presence when asking what's next
(what's next?)

Where I'm Suppose to Be

She left quotes in recorded monologues
and with each breath
I inhaled these things
lines that went straight to my brain
subconscious high that had me
hanging out with a star on Earth
multiply these verses
so we can play their parts
through different scenarios
cameo appearances on a timeline
finding ways to spark opportunities
between you and me
that's space to embrace
a little something like a cuddle
which might be, a bit much
but not enough to stop these thoughts
these vibes I rode in on
to a song coming from your lips
soothing my ears
and it appears I am
where I'm supposed to be,
enjoying the present moment
of you.

Restoration
(a lesson to self)

Solitude healing just hits different
1-2 combos that land
exactly where it hurts,
nevermind your attitude
this tool moves just as rude if necessary
finding what's buried deep down in an abyss
but this one, it just don't miss
cause what's left of tears you're still drowning in
is where the fire begins
burning the past
holding this heat
a unique experience that wasn't meant for anyone
but you,
you could pray all you want
solicit to the stars, moons or intergalactic beings
that seemingly brings no answer,
reeking of a love turned hate
while amongst the masses
but can't find not one person to relate
yet here you are shaken to the core
once making way on a journey so promising
but didn't know what you were walking in
on - from - to
thought you'd be due a solid
a common courtesy
but that left right around the time
sense was known by the same first name,
just think

you came here with the best intentions
traveling through millennia
only to be stuck in a repeated timeline,
ancestors watching from the stands
past lives on the sidelines
not knowing if they should criticize
or they realize you're about to make it
and what's that,
is that intuition whispering loudly
is that pain you complain about in your belly
really a gut feeling your avatar
was programmed to think of differently
to the point, you've trusted more
in some bullshit taught to you by broken records
so your feet said fuck it and joined in on the dance
got your, heart pumping
sending SOS's to a clouded creative room
asking you to wait, just have patience
this isn't how the story is to be finished,
self is no longer to be ignored
and the inner you begins to radiate from your chest
a depth that went from hellish
to a gentle universal kiss between the matrix
and your forehead
now you're remembering, awakening
to the fact that you've never been alone
all this time you've been experiencing a restoration
a soul trip
for the sake of an understanding

beyond limited mindsets
commanding one's way to fulfillment
with no need to look back when living in the now
and embracing what's here
it's, the divine timing of perfect imperfection
all in the effort to believe in this power
called love.

Remembering

Stop and listen
listen to colors not known on a spectrum,
so soft and gentle
like loud poetry
I'm noticing,
I'm noticing that this love
is unconditional
wrapped in warmth that flows
from pole to pole
although I can't find it's beginning
and never want it to end
I'm remembering
a mixture of sorts
life packed in boxes labeled eternity
imagine holding on to that
it's that,
undisclosed reaction
only a spirit could hug
what happens when you move above
cloud nine, one too many
there's plenty of fish in the sea
unless we're talking about
the black one
you know, the one full of salt tears
let me, not get too far fetched
or so out of reach
you forget that we're here to remember
here to tell the tale
of a starseed
that indeed seeks to breach

darkness with light
remembering that
fact checks bounce when talking with
I Am
and I put that on the culture
moving above and beyond
yet having to go below and within
to find this
nameless entity that resembles me
and she
and he
and you
cause who would have thought
without thinking
we'll call it unconscious
obnoxious that few will teach you that
fiction in facts
and with that
we are remembering
beautiful
resort to powers of stars aligned
combined into a rhyme
find the way to speak to the hand
that's written since the invention of time
signed on skylines
designed by the divine
defines the shine brought to you now
given to yours from mine
make sure to pull each other up
when climbing on the vines

intertwined with close encounters of the third kind
you'll find behind the mind
lies memories of 1990
where we can unwind.

Oh Snap

Don't snap for me
snaps snap me back
to flashbacks of 12th grade poetry class
you know what, fuck that
I prefer claps
and not the STD trap
perhaps you can level with me
I get that you might want to show appreciation
and I'm not debating at energy received
when I breathe lyrics into your spirit
you feel it and want to hear this
next line so you're inclined
to smack palms with fingertips
for the benefit of hearing my next rhyme
but really, hear me out
snaps are in fact a tactic
used as verbs in words
nerds like me wordsmith them to
snap back, snap that, snap after daps
while taking snaps with a device that
I tap for boom bap raps
but, before we go too far back
let me snatch and jack up your attention
listen Linda, listen
I'm a poet that needs to mention
I need extensions from two hands repeatedly
beating each other excitedly
happily, why would I want to be
haphazardly greeted in my speech

each week by word geeks
that seek to meet me with such enthusiasm
brain-gasm that has the reactions of
"mmmm" "whew" "damn"
I am on one and
it's that simple, that sudden
when I break in two
or bite into the meat of it
does it really matter
as I scatter thoughts under my
mad hatter poet persona
bona-fide, the look in my eyes
might give snapshots of the genius inside
that's borderline, personified
crazy, and maybe
I'm taking this too far
making more out of this than what really is
kinda like I just…snapped
you know what, fuck that
cause snaps snap me back
to 12th grade poetry class
that's a flashback
so for me, don't snap.

Incarnate

From the dust where I've come
a sun returns
a star that's run
it's course, a coarse path
made to blaze ways
to shine bright
giving off light
within the darkness of self,
here's the reasons to believe
starseed now planted
in Earth, giving birth
to love
in circumstances
and situations
that define purpose
for those things patiently waited on
weighted in
hope, faith, peace, joy
the basic instructions
played out
in all forms conceivable
no matter the belief
freely, willingly
to ensure that
we do more than just exist
we uplift consciousness
so unconditional is not just dreamed
it's believed
agreed upon

so despite the setting sun
we're found very much alive
realize now, it's our time
to rise…
rise…
rise…
rise…
rise…
rise…
rise…
rise…
rise…
rise…
rise!

About The Author

Billy Williams, Jr. was born to write poetry. Poetically knows as B-Dot and One Poetic, the life as a poet all started because of a girl back in 7th grade. Seeing he had a gift with words, he began to use his energy to produce poetry that spoke to various genres.

Hailing from Raleigh, North Carolina, Billy is a poet, educator, coach, gamer, streamer, content creator and inspirer. A Story of a Starseed is Billy's nineth book of published poetry, with more poetry books to be released in the near future.

If you want to find out more information about Billy's upcoming books, you can contact him by way of e-mail at
onepoeticgamer@amazulugaming.com
or sending a message to him from the following website www.amazulugaming.com. If you wish to know more about his gaming/streaming life, check him at www.twitch.tv/onepoeticgamer.

Social Media Contacts

Poetry Blog: www.amazulugaming.com
Instagram: Onepoeticgamer
Twitch: www.twitch.tv/onepoeticgamer

AmaZulu Gaming, LLC

Poetry Books Written By One Poetic

Poetic Superhero

Everybody is looking for a hero. Poetic Superhero is here for you.

The I prElude I

In order to find we, HE must find himself before finding SHE.

His Emotions Released

This is written for Her…I'm glad I finally got Her attention.

School Dad

Poetry inspired by 16 years of working as an educator in elementary, middle and high school.

the Book of HER

33 poems for HER.

The Poetic Verse - My Book of Rhymes

When I feel the flow, I let go with words.

Excommunicated (A Bard's Tale)

Exit wounds given by another can lead to one's salvation.

A Bit More Than a Muse

When she's a bit more than friend but hasn't recognize his energy yet…or so he thought.

Spoken Word By One Poetic

A Story of a Starseed

I wrote this for me…and her…and us.